New Moon
Renaissance

New Moon Renaissance

Marie Hague

gatekeeper press™

Columbus, Ohio

New Moon Renaissance

Published by Gatekeeper Press
2167 Stringtown Rd, Suite 109
Columbus, OH 43123-2989
www.GatekeeperPress.com

ISBN (paperback): 9781662920011

I wouldn't have been able to do this without the unconditional love and support of my husband and children. Thank you for encouraging me to follow my dreams and not to stop until I am proud.

"Poetry, I feel, is a tyrannical discipline. You've got to go so far so fast in such a small space; you've got to burn away all the peripherals."

Sylvia Plath

Mothers
How often do we lie and say,
"They complete me"
When the truth is
We are broken
And desperately pick up pieces
Hopeful to fill in the gaps
And while some of these pieces are love
Pride
And admiration
Some are fear
Uncertainty
And isolation
New pieces come together to form
An unfamiliar mosaic of our
Past, present, and future.
Someday the glue binding these pieces will weaken
But the selfless love we gave without question
Will be returned and put us
Back together.

Had this happened to me
His confidence
And dignity would be
Scattered in pieces.
Crime scene clean up
Would have been called
For his bloody emotions
Lying in heaps.
The forgiveness you exude
Makes me feel guilty
Because in this situation
All I would feel is
Hate.

Was it the beveled edge of the needle or quill that drew me to him?
Beveled.
Sharp.
Like the fine words he spoke that stuck in my skin.
Was it his melodic medicine that numbed my thoughts
And stole my courage?
Words that grew like poppies between his teeth with
Breath that lulled me into this complacency.
I could never argue with a voice like that.

Her calico soul,
Cloaked in foxglove.
His red rose passion,
Silk but artificial.
Oleander grows upon his tongue.
Bleeding hearts on a vine.
Shame like stinging nettles.
Wilt. Fade. Nurture.
Rise, Lotus. Renaissance.

As you wiggle your toes for the first time in centuries
Allow yourself to reach down below
Admire the fertile earth nurtured by your tears.
Enjoy the snapping of roots that once bound you in place
Limiting your growth.
Feel the otherworldly wind as it loosens the past
And sloughs it off into the breeze freeing untouched nerves,
anxious to feel once again.
Dance freely across the sylvan landscape as your body recalls how
to move on its own.
Feel the moss give and accept your weight in ways unfamiliar.
Take in the warmth as the sun radiates with the promise of a new day.
Decisions, like paths to new worlds,
Some with oceans
And some fields,
Are yours to make in due time.
But for now, please walk, unhurriedly.
Marvel at the wildflowers that grow in your footsteps
As the seeds of possibility scatter from your soul.

We mock her daily mantras
And scoff at her fresh starts
And her new beginnings as the
Bullet points line her resolutions
Day after day.
We laugh as she passes
Her head held high.
Assisted by an
Inspirational crutch
Vague and flowery words she believes
Speak to her.
Sunset brings acceptance of failure.
Sunrise brings a new promise.
She is all of us.

The poetic mind like
A hive.
Incessant buzzing
No direction.
No center
No calm
Overwhelming and loud.
Such beauty in knowing that
Something so sweet
Comes from
Such raw chaos.

There are nights when she throws herself to the floor
Just to see the pieces shatter. Scatter.
Some nights she meticulously glues each piece
Exactly how she remembers it.
How it should be.
Some nights she experiments with
New shapes and styles
Because maybe, just maybe
She'll work better. Feel better. Be better.
Some nights she just sits and stares
At the pieces. Broken. Sharp.
Wondering what went wrong.
But when the night fades into morning sun
She picks up those pieces
And forces them into some semblance of familiarity
For tiny feet must be safe from her shards
As they dance upon these floors.

Intention and creativity.
Prisoners trapped by exhaustion and apathy.
Their only means of escape are the dull, bloody fingernails
Scratching for eternity,
Boring small pits into the walls of the mind
Until you set free the shackles
Allowing innovation to abscond into the unseen.
Inspiration comes and goes like an unappreciated lover.
Watch it walk out the door with one last wistful glance
But remain seated and unmoved.
Wrists, limp with atrophy.
What use is it to pick up a pen
When only such fodder pours forth?
Past words hang against the wall as if
Shadow figures reaching for new life.
Desperate for fresh words
The same way one sucks the tip of a dry pen
Desperate for fresh ink.

One of these days
You're going to look beyond the
Tired eyes
And unkempt hair.
You're going to smooth out the wrinkles
With a wry, knowing smile and then
You're going to embrace the chaos
And realize that
Motherhood is the most beautiful thing you have ever worn.

I am all or nothing.
Always.
Moving too fast.
Never knew how to pace myself.
I think it's time I sit down, once a again
And rewrite the expectations
That I will never live up to.

I am afraid of what you think.
All of you.
I once paid for someone,
No better than me,
To evaluate and
Judge my words.
The words I already knew were capable of evocation.
And yet here I am
Trembling
Still desperate to share
Myself.

My eyes are yours
As well as the second hand smile
And the dimple on my right cheek.
Yours were rarely used and unneeded.
You donated my unruly, dark curls and
My temper and penchant for exaggeration.
But these emotional scars,
You handcrafted, just for me
By ripping your lazy
Contribution from my DNA.
These scars won't fade the same as
The silver breaks in my skin.
And decades later
They are still a reminder that half of me
Is out there
Capable of existing without any of me.

I burn bridges for my safety.
I salt the earth for my sanity.
Each apology removes one stitch
Too Soon.
I am creating some distance.
I am gaining perspective.
I am breaking familial cycles.
I am healing.

Woman.
The human embodiment of
Touching a sunrise.
Hopeful. Raw.
Moving with a backbone like
A strong cup of coffee.
Confident.
Seductive.
You're a day of
Endless permutations with each sip
They drink from you.
A celestial body
With a face made up of
Zodiacs.
Gemini eyes
Of both purity and desire.
A Picses mouth promising devotion
Dressed in Scorpio smile, a silent vow of passion.
A feral mind with wild dreams.
Eloquence and sincerity in every breath.
Embrace what you've been given
What you are.
Woman.

Us poets,
We take the ugly chaos
And make it beautiful.
Dress it up
And share it like
Fashion on a runway.
But in the end, even we go home
And remove our clothes to
Expose the truth.
Keep it coming.
Grind out the words.
But keep it pretty.

The promises made guide us like a lighthouse
Amidst a dark, stormy sea.
Our lack of self preservation
Paddles us in a worn and patched life raft.
Waves of better judgement work against us
And impede our progress.
We grow tired and weak
Beneath our selfless desire to please.
We ignore past broken promises
Scattered like bodies
On jagged rocks.
One of these days we will learn.
One day we will hang up our oars
And accept that life is better without tears
On dry land.

She's somewhere between
A tall poppy
And shrinking violet.
She longed to be the wildflower
But settled for common weed.
What she doesn't realize is
She's a lotus
Rising up and
Breaking free.

To my daughters,
Don't ever dull your sparkle
To appease another.
Never set yourself on fire to warm someone else
And then apologize for burning too brightly.
Remember where you came from.
A woman who meticulously created
Your every molecule from scratch
With such care and intention.
Keep dreaming
And dream big, my darling girls.
I'll be right here
Holding the ladder steady
While you climb to the stars.

I had a dream once
To set hearts on fire with words.

It's been almost three years
And the cherry blossoms still bloom on time
And the birds still remember to sing.
Maybe Spring time forgot that you're gone.

I created you
Knowing my body would never let me
Keep you.
I brought you to life
Knowing my body would never let you live.
Cracked eggs.
Empty nest.
Recurring
Shattered dreams.

The moon is beautiful but she lies.
She cannot stand alone.
Cosmic cosmetics
As she absorbs and reflects a glow
That is not her own.
You ohh and we ahh
As she shifts and changes
Manipulating her celestial body
Into something you want to see.
What you need.
She shrinks herself
As your eyes widen.
You'll grow tired of her
Ethereal crescent shape
And she will fade away
Until she regains a grasp on herself
Reinvention
Shifting in a new direction.

If only
I had
The strength
To show you
Every word
I've ever written.
You'd never be able to look me in the eyes
Again.

Amidst all the chaos and noise
My heart will always settle
When face to face with yours.

I can still hear the metallic scraping
Of your spoon against ceramic
As you stirred your tea.

When I was a little girl
I worked so hard
To make you proud
But all you saw
Was the dirt on my face
And the rips in my knees.
Days in and days out
The criticism was
Never constructive.
Each word
A new chink in my armor.
I'm a grown woman now,
No thanks to you.
But I still can't bring myself
To dismantle the baggage
You meticulously packed
Just for me.

There is no serenity
Like Sunday morning coffee
While I softly whisper
My dreams for the future
With you.

No matter the phase of the moon
I remain whole.
My capacity for bullshit,
However,
Wanes more and more
By the day.

Every kind word you speak to me
Plants itself like
A seed deep in my heart
Until flowers erupt
Pushing themselves
Between my ribs
Filling me with self-worth
And a gentle benevolence
For the person I once
Kept hidden
For fear that my ideas
And my dreams would not
Make any sense.
It is because of you
And your words that
Flow freely like merciful waters
That nourish and empower
The garden that is now blooming within me.

I can remember a mess of raven curls
Falling down into my tear stained
Alabaster face.
Standing there
Waiting.
In a faded,
Floral,
Flannel nightgown.
Breathing in the scent of
Those musty, orange drapes.
Waiting.
My tiny nose pressed against the window.
An anxious circle of condensation
Coming and going with my breath.
Waiting.
Overcome with pins and needles.
A preemptive numbing for the future.
It happened every time
I went to the window to wait for you
To come home, Dad.
But you never did.

If you think
Your tears are bitter
You should
Taste my ink.

Those who are not like us,
The tolerant,
Do not understand
Just how brightly
The fires
From the bridges we burn
Light the paths
To our freedom.

We're breaking cycles.
Strength in your vulnerability.
Beauty in my decisiveness.
Growth in our communication.
This is why we work.
This is why we'll last.

You're dwelling, my dear.
I warned you.
Just visit,
But do not take up residence
Here in this pain.
You started to grow
But the shock of
Opportunity
And a fresh start was
Too much to bear.
You pick at the scab
That had started to heal.
You always did
Find solace
And familiarity
In blood
Under your fingernails.

At times femininity feels like an insect,
Pinned to a board
And displayed beneath glass.
A specimen,
Splayed and
Labeled.
Fragile and hollow,
Left to be observed
And judged.
Nothing but a list of parts
Lacking movement and direction.
Gawked at, grimaced at.
Who does this to us?
Why do we let them?

I'm not really sure what you want me to say.
It really was all your fault.

We were a rock and he was a hard place.
You told us that.
But you always chose that hard place
Because that's where you drew your
Self-worth.
Beneath the weight of a man.
It didn't come from the beings you
Built from scratch
With your own blood and bones.
No, we were the rock.
The deadweight of motherhood
That held you back.
Decades have passed.
Nothing has changed.
You still wedge yourself
Beneath that hard place and
Allow your life force to be drained
In the name of "love."
While you watch us sink
Like rocks.

Is it a cliche that I still blame you
For my shortcomings?
Did you know that
I curse your name
Every time I attempt to
Unpack the baggage you left?
Was the praise intentionally withheld
Or was your silence a result of your
Own dysfunctional upbringing?
Was happiness a finite commodity
And were you afraid of running out?
Did we feel like a punishment
Or a privilege?
Are you even listening?

These pale silver lines are proof of
Just how much internal growth I can withstand.
My enlightenment,
So vast and yet, I accommodate.
Each delicate groove is a lesson I've learned.
The softest of sagacity lingers beneath this skin.
My body, it swells and it stretches with wisdom
And I will never break.

Eyelids scrape over
Tired eyes
That feel like sandpaper.
Still she rises
And puts one foot
In front of the other.
Immune to caffeine with
The weight of the world
Upon this crumbling keystone.

Somehow a narcissistic nihilist,
This queen of decay.
All she has left to cling to
Is her seat upon wilted laurels.
Smile.
And nod with pity.
Just walk away.
She's not coming down from
That beat up
Old
Soap box
Anytime soon.

You must allow yourself to break and
Enjoy the fall.
Relish in that shatter with
The deafening crash
And momentary loss of control.
Admire your shards with their sharp new
Edges.
What fits where now?
New pieces, new purposes.
You weren't born to be delicate china
But a strong mosaic
Cemented in experience.
Sweep up the dust and what no longer serves you.
One step closer to your final configuration.

Allow this
Newfound courage
To rip you wide open
And scream fearlessly and
Wildly
Into the chasm.
Growth and discomfort
Those synonymous sisters,
Will lead you on
This path.
Be mindful.
It is not linear,
And the end,
Just an everdistant horizon.

This cycle feels different.
There's a crackle in the air.
A tangible static.
A warmth.
A buzzing.
A new heart beats within.
The rhythm is courageous.
The rhythm is peaceful.
The full moon broke me.
She shattered the shell
That stunted my growth.
And now it's time to
Purge the stagnant and the stale.
Heal.
Rise and grow.
New Moon Renaissance.

I still talk to you.
And then I sit
And I wait
For what feels like eternities.
Desperate pleas shouted into
The deep well of my thoughts.
Four years worth of hollow
Barren faith.
Wounds torn open by silence.
Stitching myself back together with
Strands of hope
But the scar tissue builds
Thicker, tighter each time
Making it harder for my heart to beat.

It's an uninhibited dance among the constellations
As she scrapes her nails along the
Black velvet sky.
She prepares for her
Descent
Into the innovative abyss.
She will reemerge
With a lucent
crescent grin.
Eager for the next phase
Skipping from night to dark night.
Abundant
Limitless growth.

He spoke words that made me feel small
Unvalued
And at times, unsafe.
But his worth was ranked above my own
And I learned to live quietly
So as to not draw attention
Because when his eyes were on me
Even my silence was stolen
Mercilessly.

If our love languages are based
On what we lacked in childhood
Then that would explain
Why I am fluent in them all.

You know the thoughts
You're afraid to write down
Because God forbid,
Someone sees them?
These are the thoughts
That will forever take up
Residence in your brain
Until evicted onto paper.
You'll never move on
Until they move out.
So pack up those thoughts,
Neatly in a notebook,
Or hell,
Toss them from the
Bedroom window of your soul
And leave them scattered on the
Front lawn
For everyone to see.
Until then
Stagnation is your home.

With you
It's always
Tit for tat
And keeping tabs
Of your selfless acts.
Reminders of what you did
And what you're owed.

I hope someday
You realize the only person
Who can fill that gaping hole
In your life
Is you.
And everyone you walk
On and over
To achieve happiness
Is as understanding as
I am when you come
Crawling back
In need of coddling
And that unconditional
Comfort and support.

If I were to
Thread every letter
From every word
I've ever written
On a string like beads
And wrap myself
Head to toe
And Display my thoughts
And fears
And pain
Then dance and rattle about
Ringing like warning bells
You'd still remain oblivious
To my needs.

Remember when they taught us
That drowning doesn't always look like
"Drowning"?
This applies out of the water
As well.

Your heavy reliance
On those around you
To provide the consonants
And vowels
You need to spell out your
I N D E P E N D E N C E
Is ironic.

When you had no intention of ever waking up
And the sun rises
Yet again,
It can take a toll on the body
When all your soul needs is
To rest.

And just like that,
My darkest years will erupt from this
Seemingly infinite crescendo.
The truth will bleed from my mouth
Like a gaping wound
And everyone will know
What you've done.

And just when you were starting to feel
Comfortable,
Breaking free of the crippling
Feminine standards and ideals,
In comes the inevitable crash of insecurity
Shattering the thin glass bauble of confidence
You've kept balanced in one hand
While the other strategically hides
The body motherhood has given you.

At least once a day
I silently sob into my open hands
And mourn the daily death
Of her childhood.
With every sunset comes a new casualty
Of the little girl she once was
And will never be again.

The thing about motherhood is that
One second you're handed
A brand new soul
With familiar eyes that
You've known for eternities
And a mere decade or so later,
Give or take some years,
You're face to face
With a stranger
Reminiscent of someone
Whose heart
Once occupied the same space
As your own.
Someone whose path
You don't understand
But must blindly travel
Even when it hurts
Because the cycles we break and
The pain we release
Will broaden their futures in
Ways we cannot even imagine.
When our children feel free to
Shed their masks and bare their souls
Before us.
We must allow the fear disguised as hurt
To fall from our hearts and allow only
The connection and admiration
To take up this empty space
In which we once grew and nourished
The brave new souls walking beside us.

Whether you talk with
The sun in the morning
Or the moon at night
Both will tell you
It's alright to hide
And adjust your
Shape and
Shift your position
Until it feels just right.
Until the time comes
To change again.

The same way
A single spark
Can warm the soul
It can also burn it to the ground.

How perfectly convenient
That as two new saplings
We chose to grow upward
In the same direction
Warming our leaves
Beneath the same bright sun
And allowing our roots to tangle
Nourishing ourselves from
The same rich soil.
How beautiful to promise
To stand with the other
Season after changing season
Through fruitful years
And those more barren.
How comforting it is to know
That though we stand sturdy
And tall on our own
Our boundlessness lies in
The pollination of
Partnership.

I'm afraid to count my blessings out loud.
What if the universe hears me
And Karma catches up?

To my daughter…
My words are not meant to
Make you feel your struggle is
Not unique
And your challenges
Not your own.
I just want your to know
You don't have to suffer alone.

I am capable
Of standing on my own.
I know that much is true.
But the way that your
Love flows,
Seeping into the cracks
And fortifying every inch of me
Is proof that I will never have to.

I imagine your fingers
Like running water
Carving pathways into me
As they trace over my skin
On a voyage,
With which you are well acquainted.
My body reads like a map.
Its deep flushing
Like trails well traveled
Lead you to familiar
And favorite places.
When your touch slows
And lingers.
I settle into us
And allow you to stay for a while.

When mothers need rest
We settle for guilt.
And while the tired,
Aching
Muscular tangles
Soften and come undone
The second guessing
Ties knots
In our conscience.

I don't question if there was
Truly any abuse.
He may not have
Left any bruises
But my psyche is certainly
Scarred.

What a difference a spring breeze makes.
How it loosens the cobwebs and
Freshens the mind.

Every night I lie
Ensconced in unrealistic expectations.
Twisted, grimacing faces of each failure
Haunt my sleep.
I speak so assuredly
These words of positivity
And put on a brave face
So that other women might avoid
These nightly verbal self flagellations.
A feminist martyr
But the truth is my
Long mental list of shortcomings
Is born without effort
And rolls off my tongue
And then off of my bed into
Puddles on the floor.
I tell myself I will skip over
The pools of insecurity.
But as the sun rises I find myself
Splashing about and soaking my ego
In the dregs of yesterday's second guessing.
I'll stand before you all once again
As she who knows no self doubt
And I will lift you up
Above the sun
And the clouds
With all of the strength I can muster
So that you may never see
Just how much my knees quake
And threaten to buckle
Beneath the weight of my support.

Poetry exists deep in my bones.
My marrow produces words
The same as it does each red blood cell.
And just as these cells
Give me life
So do these words.
Tearing the skin
Runs red with fresh blood
Time and pressure can clot a wound.
Tearing the soul
Onto paper
Words pour.
No time nor pressure
Can stanch this flow.
Let it run its course
Until the ink runs dry.

I think I write better than you.
Maybe not before
But definitely now.
Your recent accolades
Have made you lazy.
Your words are lackluster,
Factory productions.
Just word counts and page numbers.
You've taken advantage
Of our desperate need for poetry
To exist out there in the world.
You may have three books now,
But I think I write better than you.

I settle in.
There's a meditative buzz,
A rush of adrenaline.
The pain is washed away
With the promise of new
Art to display.
I add color
And draw attention
To my body
And laugh in the faces of those
Who tell me I should
Be small.
Dainty.
Take up less space.
Never.
Did you know
Tattoo means a rhythmic tapping?
Like the steady beat of contentment
Inside of my heart
As I settle into
All of me.

I'm trying to unravel past trauma
And all of the hope for my future
But the fear and motivation are tied in a knot
So tight
That I'm not sure which thread
I'm picking at.
The juxtaposition of that
Frightened little girl
And this brave woman,
Brimming with intention,
Is an overwhelming enigma
And at times I'm not sure
I'm qualified to solve this riddle.

I think now she realizes
How easy it was for me to leave home
And how her stone cold
Emotional neglect
Made me independent
To a fault.
How the way
She shamed me for needing help
Made me strong
But bitter.
I think now she feels the
Resentment she helped me craft
By never being around
But always having an opinion.
A criticism.
A judgement.
The joke is on her though
Because I am here.
She is there
And it will always be that way.

You were a
Red flag friendship.
I ignored the little things
For the sake of convenience.
Then I took a step back
And with a new perspective,
I allowed myself to slip away.

It took decades
To fall in love with
the woman in the mirror.
I'm not willing to risk
This relationship
For the few minutes of
Daily self depreciation
Your empty friendship
Needs to survive.

Sunday morning love
Bodies
Entwined like the
Coffee rings on the nightstand.
So slow,
Breath,
And movement.
Sharing whispers
Of shared dreams
Between
Shameless morning kisses.
This isn't a Saturday morning
Kind of love
Playing a staccato conversation
On the way out
The door.
Words and sighs
Flow mellifluously
On Sunday mornings.

Mother Moon,
With her glow of
Admiration
Shimmering
Down below.
Fragile crystals
Blanketing the
Brittle
Blades of grass.
A gentle wind knocks down
The last remaining autumn leaves
From the skeletal trees.
They skitter softly
Across the frozen Earth.
She sighs and smiles
Sleepily.
Winter is here.

I suggest
You make peace with your heart
And get comfortable in your soul.
They're not going anywhere
Anytime soon.

Pause.
Regain your breath
Reign in your heart
Retain your soul.
Adjust your expectations.
Now, proceed.

Am I imagining
That our relationship was stronger
Than it was?
Is that why you don't visit me?
No dreamland drop ins,
Or strategically placed
Feathers or
Coins?
Just the ache
That holds your shape
In my heart.

Like the sea
To the moon
I succumb to the
Pull of your magnetism.

Words are always there to
Bear the burden
When the soul cannot.

There are some men
Who want to shrink us down,
Requiring us to
Take up less potential.
They push to infantilize us
With bare skin and an
Agreeable demeanor
Denying us our
Birthright to age with
Grace and Wisdom.
But women...
With lifetimes of insight and
Awareness
Passed down from generations
With bodies of Mother Earth that
Stretch
Crack and
Crumble.
Swell and Flood.
Any man should feel
So lucky to exist
Within reach of
Our infinite depths.

It's not about
Severing ties
When their presence
No longer serves
You.
This is not a selfish action.
It's acknowledging
That you've outgrown
The friendship and you are
Choosing to grow
Beyond the
Fragile,
Porcelain shell their
Stunted growth has
Settled for.

I hate that I look like you.
The older I get
The more I struggle
To find the girl who
Once resided in
Hopeful brown eyes
With plans to go further and do more
Than you had ever dreamed of
For yourself.
But what's left on most nights
Is that familiar
Tired face
Threatening me with
Wrinkles and disappointment.
I managed to change
My path and give myself a future,
Unlike you,
But I can never make this face
My own.

"Are you okay?
It's been a while since you last posted anything."
Were the last words I sent her
Way too late.

The times you weren't around
To nurture and raise her
She looked to the sky
And saw the moon.
And while those lessons
Were always in transition
At least they were consistent.

Sometimes
You let them win
The argument
Because the hill you're on
Isn't worth dying for
But the preservation of the relationship
Just might be.
Sometimes, when you take a step back
It's likely you'll see the shape of
"You're right."
Is the perfect fit
For the chink in their armor.

I want to shake some of
You
Until your worth
Clicks into place
And you realize just how much,
And for how little and how long
You've been settling.

Next time
Around I want to be
Born as
The Moon.
God knows I've spent
Enough time
In this life learning
To shrink myself into
Nothing
And starting over
Again and again.

There are never too many
Poems or
Too many
Books.
There is no competition to succeed
Among writers.
Our very existence depends
On each other.
We create and present
Our works like treats
Displayed in
An adept array.
They devour our words
And hunger for
More.
One cannot subsist
On a single page alone.

Day in
And day out
We remain contentedly
And unapologetically
In love.
And for that
I have no shame.

They say we're all made of stardust.
But not you, my dear.
You taste far too sweet
To consist of just remnants of rock
Suspended within
A whisper of death.

To the moral quandary of motherhood…
It's not easy,
Allowing yourself to be present.
Living in the moments
Is a cliche
Until you do it.
It's like when time slows down
And the Universe
Sits back
And can finally inhale
And get that deep breath
She needs to fully appreciate
What she's been gifted.

What you see are
Petals,
Fine and delicate.
Easily plucked and wilted.
What you don't see are
Roots,
Hidden deep in the earth
Steadfast and nurturing.
Just wait until you see
The growth and
Seeds.
Creation,
Culmination,
Going as far as the wind
And a whim
Will carry her.

I was flipping through
Old journals and
Poring over all of my work
And I think it would be
Lovely to take every
Word I've ever written and
Fill the bath with my letters,
Both consonants and vowels,
And soak in the feelings
I bled from myself
Like brothers consecrating
A vow.
To linger and reabsorb
The feelings of rage
And lust and fear
And pride until my skin
Grows pruny and saturated
With new permutations of feelings
I cannot let go of while the useless moments
I've outgrown swirl down the drain
Never to be reworked and rewritten again.

It comes in waves,
The grief.
No matter how much distance
I manage to put between
The shore and my heart
It always finds me.
The subtle ripples grow bigger
And more powerful
As they wash over me.
Pulling me under.
I'm left gasping for breath,
For a moment of peace
As sense memories
Pool in my lungs
Burning from lack of air.
On some days,
I fight to stay afloat
Thrashing about,
Grasping for distractions.
Other days
I succumb to your loss and allow
Myself to be torn apart by
The riptide and
Spat out,
Washed ashore in scattered pieces.
And then,
With what strength I can muster
I gather myself and carry on
But not without one final glance
At the shipwreck in my rearview.

The winter sun has never
Received proper
Appreciation.
Her subtle beauty
Deserves to be admired.
Desaturated colors and
Soft light
That's only shone
On what's important
Preserving her energy
Until she can,
At last,
Lower herself
Into the sleepy descent
And drift away
To gently warm another
Distant day.

Two decades later
And my body is still
Overcome with
Yearning
When it senses a shift of
Molecules
you enter the room.

You were so angry
And so weak.
Every time you
Lost control
And fell apart
You left shards
In my path.
Trauma like
Splinters deep in my skin
Remind me
Of what I'm missing
But safe from,
Without you in my
Life.

Don't confuse the meticulous curls
And immaculate lipstick
For someone who aims to
Please anyone
But herself.
It's all velvet and lace,
Poison and judgement
Over here.

I'm going to stick it out,
Just this one time,
Because I am curious to see
What it feels like
To succeed.

Why would I
Bend and force myself
To fit into
Your labels
When I walk naked and free
Of your stylized expectations
In self love and acceptance?
Why would I cut away at my
Body,
My worth
To make myself small enough for
You to carry me within your pocket
Like a possession
When I am capable of housing
The expanse of infinity
In a single heartbeat?

There comes a point
In the exhaustion
When a person no longer
Fears dying.
The need to stop,
To rest,
To sleep
Is so overpowering.
Certainly,
Perseverance
Is more painful
Than death.

I was never
Daddy's little girl.
I was an inconvenience,
A monthly payment.
Somedays, I am curious
Which parts of my adult life
Would be different
If you had stuck around,
If I had mattered just a little bit
More.
I bet I'd have less to write about.
So, thanks for that, Dad.

It's funny how we look to nature for inspiration
When that nagging,
Gnawing,
Picking of a hangnail
Is where the true influence lies.
The description of a sunset
A rose
And crashing waves
Could never compete
With the reason we
Dig and dig
At our own bodies
To distract us from the pain
Raging on the inside.

So many have asked
How passion remains
Nearly 2 decades later.
We smile knowingly,
As usual sharing the exact same thought.
I guess they've never know
The kind of familiar hands
Capable of eliciting screams
That rip open mundane skies
While proud whispers of ancestors
Trickle down with blessings of love
And future.

I won't bore you with cliches
Of tiger stripes
Or battle scars from winning wars
Or birthing humans with futures and souls.
But I will have you know,
I am enough.
I've cried so often
But still not enough to wash away
This grief.

I've tried and tried to
Rewire my brain
To live without you
But the urge to call you
Still remains.
No feathers
No cardinals
No heavenly dimes
Will ever fill the void.
There will forever be
An ache
Of your shape
In my heart.

I refuse to rot with you
Here in this self deprecating ditch.
Your indignation is suffocating and
Reeks of patchouli and disappointment.
I'm setting roots and moving
Onward
And upward.
I plan to grow.
I plan to thrive.
If you ever loosen your grip on
Stagnation
You can find me in the sky.

Don't laugh
But I live in constant fear
That the angels are going to steal you
From me
And keep you
As their own
Because I truly believe you are
Too good and
Too pure for this world.
My only solace
When that thought
Interrupts my day
Is knowing that nothing
Between us has ever gone
Unsaid.

I burn bridges for my safety.
I salt the earth for my sanity.
Each apathetic apology
Removes one stitch
Too soon.
I am creating some distance .
I am gaining some perspective.
I am breaking familial cycles.
I am healing.

There are days when I feel
Strong like a sturdy
Earthenware platter
Capable of catering to many,
Many people.
Then there are days when I feel like
A flimsy, paper dessert plate
Collapsing beneath the weight
Of a single serving.

Do you think I'll
Recognize your face
When my spirit returns home?
I once knew your soul completely
But your body was never mine to hold.
The grief and heartache linger,
Having never held your hand.
But looking back
I find solace
Knowing the angels had bigger plans.

What gives me the right
To complain about this
Charmed life?

I spent the morning
Sitting in my car
Drinking coffee
Watching the rain
And listening to bitter women sing.
Just in case you were
Wondering how
Extra I am today.

I hope you read this one day
And realize your bitterness fueled my success.
Your petty reactions
Ignited my creativity
And your manipulative ways
Provided endless inspiration.
Thanks for the trouble.

Made in United States
North Haven, CT
09 April 2022

18054289R00082